Shoot
the
Messenger

A Quest to Communicate Well

Mike Vayda

ISBN: 978-0-9834949-0-4

Printed in the United States of America

"Let's face it.

Some people have a way with words.

And others…uh…not have way, I guess."

— Steve Martin

Acknowledgements

To those who are masters of the art,
thank you for teaching me.

To my students and clients,
thank you for the privilege of your attention.

To the arrogant, unprepared and uncaring speakers,
thank you for the motivation.

To Lisa Horn, thank you for being my right arm
across cities, countries and continents.

To Mike Miclon,
thank you for the brainstorming sessions.

To my kids, who listened to every draft,
bless you for your enthusiasm.

And, to my ever-patient wife…
my dear, this book, at last, is dedicated to you.

Why this book is worth the money
(and maybe a bit more).

As the saying goes, I've got good news and bad news.

First, the bad news. It's getting a great deal harder to communicate. Whether it's a large event, a small group discussion, or just a personal conversation, you've got a challenge ahead of you.

Why? Because people have rediscovered the power of *shooting the messenger*.

Just a few years ago, an audience would sit politely through almost anything. Today, they won't hesitate to tune out *within minutes*. This is especially true if they sense a speaker who is unprepared, uncaring, or uninteresting.

In ancient times, messengers like that would have met with the sharp end of an arrow. Today, technology is the weapon. Speakers are looking up to find a sea of heads bowed over glowing screens. Not as deadly as the old days, but painful nonetheless!

Technology is the weapon; it's also the competition. Each day, people are bombarded with thousands of messages. *Why should they pay attention to yours?*

I have a unique perspective. For the past twenty-five years, I've been a public speaker, presenter coach, media creator, and event producer. I've been on stage, backstage...even built the stage. I've experienced audiences on five continents. What is <u>my</u> message?

*Learn to communicate **well**...or else.*

Now, here's the good news.

It *is* possible to keep your audience engaged, even in the face of encroaching technology and short attention spans. The secret is learning just six basic principles.

And yet, who wants to read a how-to manual to learn them? If I were you, I'd rather read a story. So, that's what you have in your hands. *Shoot the Messenger* is a fable, set in a medieval world. It's about a man who travels to a hostile kingdom to deliver a message and learns to communicate well...eventually. By reading this story, you can learn the principles too, and they can equip you to communicate to any audience, any size, anywhere.

That's why the book is worth the money (and probably more.)

These are indeed difficult times to be a communicator, but it's still possible to move people with your words. When you do, there's really nothing like it. My hope is that this story will help you learn, like Crier, how to deliver information in the best manner possible, a way that you can be proud of.

Through this book, may you discover the noble calling of Messenger. And may you experience the joy of communicating *well*.

— Mike Vayda

Prologue

In all her years, the queen had never witnessed such a bad presentation.

The Messenger stood before her. He had a horrified look on his face—and well he should. He was an odd little man. His balding pate was shiny, and the random tufts of red hair were matted with sweat. His clothes were muddy and ripped, and his shirt was actually *smoking*. She noted with mild curiosity a small, withered flower pinned to the lapel. As her eyes moved down to his feet, she looked away. She didn't even want to see what he was standing in.

The floor glittered with shards of broken mirror. A horse, which had deposited the pile in which the man was standing, snorted and sneezed from the acrid smoke hanging low in the air. The man was looking at a mangy dog, which barked and whined, occasionally stopping to scratch himself furiously. The only other sound in the shocked throne room was the occasional cough or snicker.

Suddenly, a man at the queen's right hand jumped up. He was dressed in the finest of clothes, richer even than the queen's. An older man, he still had a commanding presence. His well-coiffed hair, goatee, and curled mustache reeked of pompousness and power. A long, thin scar ran down the right side of his face. The crowded room quickly hushed.

In a loud and theatrical voice he proclaimed, "*This* is how you repay the kindness of a queen?"

He paused for effect and then slowly walked toward the little man. Glass crunched beneath his heavy boots. He waved a gloved hand at the chaos around him. "I knew from the moment you limped in here that you were trouble for our kingdom." A look of distaste crossed his weathered face, and his lip curled. "I *told* the queen—"

Here he stopped himself and bowed stiffly to the woman on the throne. "I am sorry, Your Highness. I mean no disrespect." Then he turned back to his audience again. "This...idiot is nothing but a foreigner, a spy from that little backwater kingdom of *Zackovia*." He drew out the last word, making it sound pitiful. He waited while a round of low laughter made its way across the room. Then he drew himself up to his full height and sneered at the small man. "But as Protector of the Kingdom of Brynnland, I will NOT allow this to continue. You have used up your last chance here, you inarticulate oaf, and this travesty will now come to an end. I—"

"Sit down, Hesston," the queen said quietly.

The man stopped short, shocked that he was interrupted. He paused and then said softly, "My lady, if there were ever a time to shoot the messenger, is it not now?"

The queen said nothing. She looked at the odd little man standing before her. The man was still staring at the dog. The dog, unaware of the drama, yawned.

Hesston took the queen's silence as agreement. He settled back into his chair and folded his arms. He smiled, a gleam in his ink black eyes. "I will give you a moment to make peace with your creator. And then? It will be time to say goodbye—once and for all."

The little man was known as Crier. He looked up at the queen. She was again surprised by his bright green eyes. For a brief moment, he thought he saw pity in hers.

He sighed. *Why did I ever agree to deliver this message? I should have told the king no.* He closed his eyes and thought back to that fateful day when everything changed.

As his eyes closed, Hesston rose again to his feet and yelled with glee, "Bowman! Now!"

Mike Vayda

Chapter

1

A fortnight earlier

Crier was at the pub, as usual, when the request came from the king.

It had been another long day. He was enjoying his privacy and his ale equally as he sat huddled in the corner, away from the crowds of happy townsfolk. All around him, people were talking, laughing, raising glasses, and slapping backs after a hard day's work. All except Crier.

His striking green eyes narrowed into slits as he took another drink from his mug. He wiped the back of his hand across his aging face. Perhaps, some years ago, he might have been considered handsome. But now, as he lurched into middle age, that consideration was fleeing. The constant scowl on his face, the rapidly thinning hair (shocking in its red color), the patchy beard he made no attempt to keep neat—it seemed as if he was doing everything in his power to be unattractive. He took another long swig and sighed. *Another day gone.*

A burst of laughter suddenly filled the cozy room, and he glowered in its direction. How he hated these peasants! For the thousandth time, he thought, *If I had my way, I'd have nothing to do with people—ever.*

This wish was both ironic and impossible, and he laughed bitterly as he realized it. He was the Kingdom Crier of Zackovia. His job was to report the news to the population. He did this twice each day, once in the morning and once in the evening. In the morning, he would climb the cathedral steps, ring the bell, and read the announcements. This told everyone that a new day had begun. And, in the evening, when people heard the bell and the announcements, they knew that another day had drawn to a close. Every day, he was forced to stare into hundreds of faces he cared nothing about. Every morning. Every evening. He shook his head and sighed again.

In most countries, being the Kingdom Crier was a position of great importance. Criers would report on things like mighty battles and read wonderful proclamations about heroes. But this Crier lived in the sleepy little kingdom of Zackovia, where nothing much seemed to happen at all. (There were stories, whispered by folks of a certain age, about days of old when things were a great deal more exciting. But Crier never cared enough to learn more.)

Crier hated his job. He didn't think it was important. He didn't care if people heard the news or not. He loathed looking down on their empty heads, waiting eagerly for the useless information.

As the pub filled, he nursed his ale and thought back to just an hour earlier, when he delivered the evening news. He had opened the cathedral doors, ignored the smiling monk and the scurrying children, climbed the 96 worn stone steps, grasped the rough rope, and rang the bell. As the people gathered in the square below, he cleared his phlegmy throat and began.

> Citizens. The ancient kingdom of Zackovia, ruled by Good King Owin, is at peace. Be thankful to your God for the blessings he has given.

Then, he paused and scowled at their pleasant, upturned faces. He proceeded to mumble his way through:

> This evening, we are pleased to announce the birth of young Claude to the Hopper family. Granny Smith is recuperating from her recent fall from the tree. And, tomorrow only, Farmer Griswold is offering two potatoes for the price of one when you also buy a swallow (European only).

He paused and added contemptuously, "The Crier of Zackovia says it is six of the clock and all is well."

He didn't make it easy for them to listen; he was quite terrible at his job. He would ring the bell furiously, or sometimes only once, just to annoy them. Then, he would keep his head down, pout his lower lip, and mutter his way through the message. People would crane their necks to hear, they would stand absolutely still, and they would shush their children and their animals. Even then it was almost impossible to understand what Crier was saying. It was as if he purposely was trying to keep people from hearing the news. And he was, of course.

People would turn to their neighbors and say, "Did you hear what he said? What was the baby's name? Was that an African or European swallow?" They would still be puzzling by the time he had descended the stairs. And as Crier pushed his way through the crowd on his way to the pub, he would hear them and smile a tight little smile.

At least once a day, he would overhear someone ask, "Why in the world does King Owin let *him* be the Crier? He's terrible. Why doesn't the king replace him with someone who cares?"

And frankly, Crier would wonder the same thing.

He was wondering that again as he heard the sound of breaking glass. He looked around angrily, and his eye caught a stranger sitting at the bar. She was an older woman, well dressed. He watched her curiously as she looked around the room, until her eyes found Crier. She stared at him long enough for Crier to become uncomfortable. He lowered his head and concentrated on drinking his beer. When he looked up again, she was talking to the bartender.

"Where did that Kingdom Crier come from?"

The barkeep looked at the well-dressed woman as he dried a tankard with a rough towel. He looked over at Crier and shrugged his broad shoulders.

"Who knows? He's an orphan, far as we can tell. He was raised by the nuns. Yet he hates them as much as he hates everyone else. Ungrateful..."

The woman politely ignored the string of adjectives that followed and looked over at Crier again. She had seen him deliver the news earlier. She had watched his suspicious eyes and bitter, angry frown. She noticed his ratty clothes, scruffy beard, and tufts of frizzy red hair that hadn't been combed in days. And here he was now, eyes darting from person to person, looking for someone to cross him.

"What's his name? Does he have any family now?"

The bartender finished pulling a pint and sent it skidding down the bar. "He lives alone. No one knows his name. We call him Crier because that's what he does."

"You mean because of his job."

"Well, that too," the barkeep replied as he wiped his hands on his apron. "But it's mostly because it's what he *does*. He complains all the time. So we call him Crier. He's also rude, arrogant, and a little stupid." The barkeep smiled at the attractive woman. "But that would make for too long of a name, wouldn't it?"

"Then how did he get his job? Where I come from, the Crier is an important position, and only those who are trained and skilled get to apply."

Again the barkeep shrugged his shoulders. "Our king is a wise man. But no one understands his thinking when it comes to the Crier. No one."

The woman drank her mead thoughtfully, watching Crier sitting alone. Clearly working his way toward drunkenness by now, he was staring into the distance, one hand on his pint, the other absently fingering a pathetic little flower pinned to the burlap vest. She finished her drink, thanked the barkeep, dropped a Cronin on the counter, and left.

Hours later, when Crier was well into his fourth ale, a man appeared at his table. Crier squinted up at him and saw that he was wearing the clothes of the royal guard.

"I'm not drunk enough to cause any problems...yet," he slurred.

The guard just smiled and said, "I'm not taking you to jail today, Crier. Just the opposite. The king has summoned you."

Crier almost spit out his ale. "King Owin? Why? What did I do?"

The guard raised an eyebrow and said, "You shall find out. Tomorrow, right after your morning announcements." And with that, he walked out, leaving Crier to sit and wonder.

Chapter

2

"**The Crier of Zackovia says it is eight** of the clock and all is well."

"And good riddance to all of you," he finished, more quietly, as he looked down on the good people of Zackovia.

"What did he say? Who died?" People were left, as usual, scratching their heads at what Crier had announced.

He scurried down the rough stairway of the tower, ignoring the pounding headache at each step. He glanced down at his clothes. He had put on his nicest vest (which wasn't very nice) in preparation for his meeting with the king.

He had spent a lot of time the night before mulling what this invitation from the king might mean. After his sixth ale, he had come to the conclusion that the king must be giving him a gift of some kind, most likely for his faithful service as Kingdom Crier for all these years. This morning, however, as his head throbbed, he wasn't as sure about that as he had been the night before.

He pushed his way through the crowded streets, and people called out, "It's about time you were replaced!" and "I hope the king boxes your ears for all the pain you've caused ours!" Crier ignored them and focused on trying to convince himself again of an impending reward. How much money would he receive? *Maybe it will be a knighthood—or some land!* His muddled mind raced as he threaded his way through slow moving oxcarts, ducks, and peddlers and on up the hill to the castle gates.

Now King Owin was wise and well loved by his people, and his white hair and beard were evidence of his many years of rule. He looked up as the palace guard escorted the scruffy little man into the long throne room. Crier approached and bowed, his eyes shifting from the king to the ground and back again.

"Royal Crier of the Kingdom!" the king said pleasantly.

"Just 'Crier,' sir."

The king paused. "What?"

Crier cleared his throat. "Ah, my name is Crier. I tell the news to earn a living, but I go by the name of Crier."

The people of the king's court stirred uneasily. It was not wise to be so rude before the king.

But the old king merely paused and smiled.

"Crier, then," he said gently. He studied the little man in front of him for a moment and then said, "I have a task for you." He waited until Crier met his gaze. "Are you willing?"

"Oh yes, of course," Crier said breezily, his mind working. *Task, eh? Perhaps he means to give me a choice of gifts.*

"I'm sure that I am most qual—"

The king cut him off with a slight wave of his hand.

"I did not ask if you were qualified. I asked if you were willing. This task is of the utmost importance." He leaned forward in his throne. "Will you do whatever it takes to see it through?"

"Whatever it takes?" Crier muttered and looked to the ground. This did not sound like a gift at all. What was this task that was so important to the king? Was it dangerous? Perhaps it would be best to just go back to his boring announcement-making and leave this business to someone else.

The king seemed to sense his hesitation.

"Rest assured that it is *you* who must do this, son. No one else." He sat back again. "Now. Do I have your word that you will not fail me?"

There was a long silence, and the crowd murmured. How dare this sloppy, good-for-nothing drunkard keep the king waiting? Would he be so foolish as to say no?

Meanwhile, Crier was thinking. It was widely believed throughout the kingdom that Crier was slow and dull-witted. In reality, he had a quick mind when he worked at it. He just didn't much care for work. Now, however, he was mulling over his limited options.

He had no desire to agree to anything that required risk or exertion, to be sure. Was there any way to get out of this? Then, like a flash of insight, he recalled the day many years ago when his life changed, when he was offered the job of Kingdom Crier. He had been in prison—again. "Why me?" he had asked. The jailer had shrugged and said, "I have no idea. If it were up to me, I would leave you to rot in here. But I bow to the king's wisdom." The man had eyed Crier as he sat in chains. "You would be wise to take this offer from the king. You will not get another."

His mind came back to the present. He realized that this might be a way to settle the debt he owed the king. A boring life as Kingdom Crier was still better than a life in jail. "Yes," he sighed and looked at the king. "Yes, you have my word."

"For what little that's worth," came a whisper from the back, and a snicker ran through the room. If the king heard it, he did not show it.

"Very well then," said the king. He opened his hand, and instantly someone placed a parchment there. The king then held it out to Crier as he spoke with conviction.

"This is a message. You will take it to the Queen of Brynnland. Please deliver it to her in the best manner possible, for she must receive this and act on it with haste. Do you understand?"

Oh. Crier thought. *Just a delivery of some sort.* Well, he didn't care much for travel, but if this would clear the books with the king, he figured it would be worth the trip. *Two days travel to pay a debt.* "Yes, of course, your Highness," said Crier as he took the parchment. He stifled a yawn and looked for the door. "I will hand it to the queen..."

The king was still holding the other end of the parchment.

"No, Crier," the king said, somewhat sternly. "I said, '*Deliver it to her in the best manner possible.*'" The regal old man leaned forward and waited for Crier to meet his eyes. The room was silent. "Do you understand?"

Crier paused, puzzled. *What was so difficult to understand here?* "Yes. Of course, Your Majesty. Deliver it to her."

"...in the best manner possible," the king said firmly.

"In the best manner possible," Crier repeated.

King Owin released the parchment and raised one eyebrow. "The queen does not easily suffer fools."

"Then why send Crier?" someone whispered, drawing a few quiet laughs. The king continued. "Would you like to read the message, Crier?"

Crier stifled a snort. "What? Read it? Um, no, I don't think so. No need."

The king paused. "I see. Do as you see fit, Crier. Just remember to deliver it...."

"...in the best manner possible. Yes Your Highness," Crier said dismissively. "Er, may I go now?"

"One final thing," the king said. Crier slumped his shoulders. He wanted to get this over with! "If you need help while in Brynnland, ask the monks how to find an old wizard named Campazani. Ask only the monks, no one else. Is that clear?"

Crier had been looking at the door. He looked back at the king and said, "Campa...who?"

The guard next to him swatted him across his balding head. Crier looked at him angrily. The guard said with exaggerated slowness, "Camp-ah-Zahn-ee, you dolt."

Crier rubbed his head and repeated the name in the same slow manner, "Camp-ah-Zahn-ee. I got it!"

The old king cleared his throat. Crier looked back at the king. "I will wait to hear from you as soon as the message is delivered. Godspeed to you."

Crier turned to go.

"And, son?"

Crier tried to muzzle a sigh of frustration and turned back to the king. The old man paused and looked into Crier's green eyes, as if searching for a connection. "If you do this task for me, you will be rewarded in ways you cannot even imagine."

Crier nodded dumbly, feeling awkward under the intense gaze of the revered old man. Finally, he cleared his throat and bowed clumsily.

And with that, Crier was escorted out of the throne room, through the palace, and into the courtyard, where a fine horse was waiting for him.

He grasped the reins and paused. He put the parchment into his vest and, with some difficulty, mounted the steed. He took one look back at the castle looming large over him and then galloped off toward the neighboring kingdom of Brynnland and his destiny.

Chapter

3

The next morning found Crier standing impatiently in the line of people waiting outside the throne room of Queen Abigail of Brynnland.

He was tired and dusty from the ride the day before, a bit hungover from too many Brynnish porters at the local pub that night, and grouchy from sleeping in the moldy straw behind the pub that he was thrown into earlier this morning. "Not very friendly folk, these Brynnlanders. Can't take a joke," he muttered to himself as he thought back to the night before.

To kill the time while he waited to see the queen, he looked around. The waiting hall was huge and opulent, and people were constantly walking around him, back and forth, dressed in finest silk and gold. He was quite a sight in contrast, with his peasant's clothes and pitiful vest, the faded flower attached. He clutched the parchment that contained the message from his king. For other people, it would have been intimidating. But Crier was a man who was unusually full of himself. For a little man who looked the way he did, his arrogance was certainly unwarranted. Nevertheless, he was the picture of confidence as he shifted from one foot to the other, rolling his eyes and shaking his head impatiently.

In front of him stood a monk. Crier noticed that he had red hair, like his own, except he had much more of it and it was much neater. The monk was the next in line to see the queen. Crier stood on his toes and tried to see over him into the throne room. His stomach gurgled. How long would this take? He was getting hungry.

Suddenly, a yelp of pain was heard, echoing from the room ahead of him. After a moment, two guards appeared, carrying a whimpering man between them. Crier gasped. The man was holding his right leg and moaning. And with good reason: an arrow was firmly lodged in the man's thigh!

He watched the guards drag the man past him, holding him up as his feet dragged along the tile floor. Crier paused for a moment, squinting his eyes in thought. Finally, he sidled up to the entry guard at the doorway and cleared his throat. "So...what's that all about?"

The entry guard glanced down at Crier with disdain and with a condescending sigh, said, "If the queen doesn't like what the messenger has to say, she orders him shot with an arrow. Where the arrow goes depends on how much she dislikes your message."

Crier's face paled. "Ah."

His stomach made another noise, but it wasn't from hunger.

The guard motioned for the monk in front of Crier to enter the throne room. Crier noticed beads of sweat on the monk's forehead as he went through the doorway. He strained to see around the corner, but could not.

"He has no chance," the guard muttered.

Crier said, "What do you mean?" The guard considered whether it was worth explaining and then said, "He's been trying to get the cathedral doors opened for years. The queen never budges." He looked at Crier curiously. "I would think you would be interested in that as well."

Crier snorted. "Huh? Why should I care about anything that happens here?"

The guard considered the man before him and finally shook his head in obvious disgust. "Silly of me. I should have known better."

Crier shrugged and went back to scheming. He looked up into the rafters, trying to think through what was happening. *Why did I agree to this task?* He was certainly having second thoughts now. He was busy devising a way to quietly slip away when, suddenly, there was a sharp cry. A moment later, the red-haired monk stumbled through the doorway, clutching his shoulder. Crier winced; an arrow was embedded in the monk's bicep!

He looked at Crier, and their eyes met. "She refuses to open the cathedral doors," he gasped. "She will not listen!"

Crier stared after the monk as he stumbled away. He glanced down at the parchment clutched in his suddenly sweaty hand. *I hope this isn't an invitation to a church service.*

The guard looked down at the little peasant. He sneered as he saw the faded flower pinned to Crier's vest. He reached and said, "The least you could do is get a fresh flower for the queen, you imbecile." Suddenly, Crier reached up and grabbed the guard's hand before he could touch the flower. His grip was surprisingly powerful, as was his voice as he said quietly, "Touch that, you lackey, and it shall be the last time you use that hand. Is that clear?" The guard towered over him; still he hesitated. Finally he said, "Your turn, stranger. Remember, be clear and be quick about what you have to say. The queen does not easily suffer fools."

"Yes, I've heard that before," Crier said as he released the guard's hand and stumbled forward into the throne room of Queen Abigail of Brynnland.

He couldn't help but stop and gape at the grand room. It was incredible—bigger and more impressive than the throne room of his king. Crier didn't normally notice subtle things, but for some reason—maybe it was because his blood was pumping from the altercation with the guard—he sensed sadness and decay in the room, as if the best days were over long ago. Something did not quite feel right.

Suddenly, the voice of the entry guard boomed out behind him. "Your Highness, may I present the Kingdom Crier of Zackovia with a message from King Owin the Enduring."

Crier jumped at the sound and then shook his shoulders to try to regain his arrogance. He took a breath, gathered his tattered garments around him, and walked forward. There were dozens of people standing in small groups, and they all stopped their gossiping to stare at him. People lined the sides of the red carpet that led from his feet to the throne in the distance. He sighed.

"All right then," he muttered to himself as he began to walk. "I'll just walk up, hand the queen this piece of parchment, do a little curtsey, and be on my way. Always do it with authority, I say. This is straight from a king, after all! Pretend you mean it and they'll believe it."

He passed a soldier standing at attention and unconsciously slowed his gait. The burly soldier was holding a menacing bow. A quiver of arrows was on his back. He stood stock still but followed Crier with his eyes. Crier thought he saw a trace of a smirk on his face. He swallowed and sped up his walk.

As he approached the throne, he saw that the queen was listening closely to a man at her side. The man was dressed in robes as regal as the queen's, possibly even more so. The man was speaking passionately, and as he spoke, he ran his fingers over a gold chain around his neck. As Crier got closer, he overheard him say, "...is why we must never allow the monks back into the cathedral, Your Highness. They preach against you and against the kingdom!"

Crier stood waiting for the queen to acknowledge him. As he waited, he studied her. At first glance, she looked old and tired. Although she was dressed in expensive clothes, they looked a little out of style, almost as if she didn't care how she looked. She had a faraway look in her eye as the man next to her gestured and spoke passionately. If he had to make a wager, Crier would bet that this woman wasn't very happy.

At last the man stopped talking, and with a sigh, the queen replied, "I am not so sure, Hesston. But I will trust your word on this. The doors will remain closed." The queen paused and then looked at Crier. Crier noticed she had a thin face, blond hair, and piercing blue eyes. He thought, *Well! In the old days, she may have been a bit of a looker.*

She narrowed her eyes, and in a panic, Crier thought he might have said it out loud. She lifted her chin in a haughty manner and said dismissively, "You. Crier. From Zackovia? What message do *you* have for me?"

Crier glanced at Hesston. He was an older man, coldly handsome, with a pointed goatee, a curled mustache, and a long scar across his right eye and cheek. Crier gave him his most winning smile. Hesston glowered at Crier and fingered the chain of gold.

Finding no friend there, Crier turned to the queen and smiled confidently as he cleared his throat. He stepped forward and held the parchment up high in his right hand. The room became completely quiet in expectation.

"I have here in my hand an important message from my king. The king told me that only I could deliver it to you."

He paused for effect. "So! Here I am. And...here's the message!" With some flourish, Crier swooped the parchment down and into the queen's hand. It made a small *smacking* sound.

The crowd gasped. The queen raised one eyebrow. When she did, she suddenly looked younger. Despite—or maybe because of—the look of anger on her face, he couldn't help but think, *Yes. Most definitely a looker!*

There was a long pause. Crier stood and waited, blissfully unaware of any faux pas on his part. He cleared his throat again. No one spoke. He decided to do what he did best: talk.

"Alright then! There's the message. I hope you like it. It's all there for you to read at your leisure."

No response.

"I wish you luck, health...the religion of your choice— or no religion, seeing as how you seem to hate churches and all...and good tidings to you...and...your...kin."

The queen held the parchment, looking at him. Still nothing but silence in the room. Crier decided to fill it.

"Ha! Yes. Right. If you wish to reward me for my service, there is no need. Although, if you have an extra room here in the castle, I certainly wouldn't turn it down. It's a long ride back to Zackovia, you know. So, if you would like to...offer...I would prefer a soft mattress...and...."

The queen's eyes shifted briefly from Crier to the bowman, just beyond Crier's right shoulder.

Only now did it dawn on Crier that something was amiss. He said nervously, "What? Is there something wrong with the message?"

The queen looked hard at Crier, her blue eyes looking like ice. "*This* is how you deliver a message of kingly importance?" She shook her head haughtily. "If I am so trivial to you, Crier, your message shall be trivial to me."

With that, Hesston gave a slight nod to the bowman.

Behind him, Crier heard a slow creaking sound and winced.

Chapter
4

Crier awoke to a loud yell. It sounded like a little girl in pain. He blinked and saw an old nun leaning over him. She was holding an arrow in her hand. With a start, he realized that the cry had come from him.

The nun looked over her spectacles at Crier with a tight smile on her face. "Would you like to keep this as a souvenir of your presentation to our queen?" She said to herself, "I don't think I've ever seen someone get The Nod so quickly before."

Crier groaned as he sat up and looked at her warily. She reminded him of the nuns in the orphanage back in Zackovia. He didn't like her.

"Un-believable! I can't believe she had me shot!" He paused. "And I can't believe she rejected the king's message! What is wrong with that woman?"

The nun frowned as she wiped her hands on a towel. "Don't you know anything about delivering a message to someone? Are you that daft?"

Crier shook his head dismissively. "My dear lady, I would have you know that I am a Messenger and—"

She cut him off with a snort of derision. "A Messenger?! You are no Messenger! You are nothing more than a crier. You have no right to call yourself anything until you actually deliver a message well."

Crier stopped. For some reason he couldn't explain, that stung a little. He tried to shrug it off.

"What? Fine. I am no Messenger. It is just that my king asked me to—"

She threw the towel down. "Your king? Asked you to what?"

He screwed up his face in concentration and finally, in his finest imitation of the king, said, "Please deliver it to her in the best manner possible, for she must receive this and act on it with haste." Crier looked at the nun haughtily. "And that's what I did."

The nun stared. "Obviously that is *not* what you did or you wouldn't have been shot with an arrow, would you then?" She sighed and picked up a bandage. She wrapped it around his shoulder vigorously. "You are *supposed* to be a *Messenger*. How can you be so ignorant of your *task*?"

Crier yelled, "Ow! Hey! Easy, Sister!"

He then mumbled uncomfortably, "Well, perhaps I have my own way of, uh, messenger-ing." He stood, winced, and then stretched his arms wide. "Not that it matters anyway. I'm finished! I've paid my dues. I've done my time. I've served my sentence—"

Suddenly, the nun slapped something into his open hand. "Oh good heavens, no," she said. Crier looked down. It was the parchment! "The queen has rejected your message. She has refused to accept it."

Crier was stupefied. "What? I thought...the nerve! You can't mean. You mean that—"

The old woman cut in. "What I *mean* is that you have not completed your task. I *mean* that you will have to go back before the queen again in hopes that she will accept the message." Crier stared at her in stunned silence. She said more gently, "And, I *mean* that you will not be leaving Brynnland until the task is done."

Crier sat back down. "What can I possibly do differently to get rid of this troublesome message?" He paused, felt his stomach, and then said, "Even more importantly, where can I get a pint, a pie, and a place to sleep?"

The nun shook her head. "If you're hungry, go see the monks. They're staying at an inn called The Buck in Field, just down the lane from the cathedral. They've been there ever since the cathedral doors were locked."

The nun looked around the room before saying, in a lower voice, "And as for your inability to deliver a message, I would try the Alchemist."

And with that, she showed him the door.

Chapter

5

Crier, fortified by some excellent food and ale compliments of the monks, attempted to leave Brynnland the very same evening, even though he hadn't delivered the message. As he reached for the reins on his horse, a gloved hand came down on his sore shoulder. "You have a job to do before you can think of leaving, little man." It was the towering guard from the throne room. Behind him stood a dozen of Hesston's soldiers. Crier sighed and headed back to the monks at the inn.

He passed through the square in front of the cathedral. He paused and glanced at the doors, chained and locked. He looked up at the dark stone tower that loomed over the square. He hurried down the lane to the inn.

Even though they had been booted from the cathedral and their home, the monks were more than happy to let him stay with them. They tried to cheer him up, but Crier would have none of it. He spent the evening sulking and the night grumbling in fitful sleep.

Finally, at breakfast he came to a conclusion. If he ever hoped to get back to his old life as Kingdom Crier (which was looking better and better all the time), he had to figure out what he did wrong and fix it fast. He needed to find this "Alchemist."

He asked the monks about this as he reached for another thick slab of brown bread. They exchanged glances but said nothing. Crier noticed the silence. He tried a different tack. He put down his knife and said in a pious voice, "Please, my...my brothers." A few monks rolled their eyes. Crier continued. "Fellow, er, travelers! On this...journey of, of life! If you can just point me in the right direction, I promise I won't say a word about it to anyone." Still they wouldn't answer.

He looked around for some help. He saw a red-haired monk. He was the one who had been at the castle, and his name was Patrick. His arm was in a sling. In his best sanctimonious voice, Crier said, "Would not our Lord want you to help me in this way?"

Patrick shook his head and then smiled. "Alright. I'll show you the way to Campazani."

Crier perked up. "Campazani? Camp-ah-Zah-nee?! That's the man King Owin told me to see! But he said he was a wizard, not some alchemist."

A young monk next to Crier said, "Practically the same. The things that old man can do! He knows the ancient art of mixing elements together." He drew closer and whispered. "There are even stories of him making gold!"

"All I need is a magic potion to get me back home," Crier said. "Can he do that?"

Patrick, smiled. "You'll find out soon enough, *brother*." And he began to draw a map.

Thirty minutes later, map in hand, Crier found the old shop, tucked into an alley off a tiny cobblestone street, far away from the castle. Its small windows were dust covered, and he could not see inside. The weathered sign above the door read, Coburn / Apothecary.

"What is it with all these different names and jobs?" he muttered as he approached the door and knocked.

A full minute passed before someone answered. The man who peered through the door was a very short, wiry old gent with thick spectacles, a prominent nose, and frazzled hair. He pressed his nose against the glass and looked Crier slowly over from toe to head. He squinted at Crier's vest and his eyes widened slightly. Quickly, he unlocked the door and waved him inside.

Crier looked around as the tiny man closed the door behind him. The shop was dusty but larger than it looked from the outside. A fire was ablaze in the hearth, and something was cooking over the fire that filled the room with a rich, warm smell. The room was filled with many books, quite a few cobwebs, and several glass cabinets. Crier saw that the cabinets contained dozens of vials of powders, herbs, and colored liquids.

The old man slowly eased himself into a chair and looked at Crier. The light glinted off his thick glasses. He said quietly, "Well? Why are you here?"

Crier said, "First of all, why is there a different name outside? And why are you called so many different things? And why is it so hard to find your blasted little shop?"

The man shrugged lightly. "I have my reasons for wanting to be...hidden."

Crier waited for more information. After a few moments of silence, he saw he wasn't going to get any. He also realized that the old man was not going to offer him a chair. Miffed, Crier introduced himself and told his story. He took the time to make sure the wizard knew how unfair this all was, how rude the queen was, and how bad his entire life had been. While he listened, Campazani looked into the distance, saying nothing. Crier finished by saying, "So you see, I just need some kind of potion that will, oh, I don't know, fly the parchment into the queen's hands, or blind the guards' eyes, or, um, maybe sweep me off to Zackovia on a unicorn, or...something. What do you think? Got anything like that, old man?"

Crier finished with a hopeful smile. Campazani sat quietly for some time.

Finally, he stood up and shuffled over to a corner where he found a small stool. Crier watched as the old man, grunting as he bent over, picked up the stool and slowly made his way toward him. He put the stool down next to Crier and reached out his hand. Taking the cue, Crier held out his arm, and Campazani leaned on it to slowly climb the two steps, making him about eye level with Crier. Then, the old man raised him arm and whacked Crier firmly on the forehead.

"Ow!" Crier exclaimed.

The old man scowled and peered into Crier's eyes through his glasses. "You do not even understand the *concept* of being a Messenger, do you?" He shook his head slowly and sighed. "I do not know if I can help you. It is clear that you are proud and lazy and unwilling to learn the skills that you need."

Campazani waited until Crier offered his arm, and then he climbed off the stool and slowly carried it back to the corner.

Crier rubbed his head and muttered, "King Owin said you would help me, not *hit* me."

When Crier said this, the old man stopped and turned his head to one side.

He sighed a deep sigh, walked back to Crier and wagged a crooked finger in his face. "You do not deserve this. For your king—and only for your king—will I do this."

"Finally!" Crier said and smiled happily. "It's about time someone gave me a fair shake in this godforsaken kingdom." And to himself, he thought, *I'll be back at the old pub in time for a pint tomorrow night!*

Campazani frowned. "You certainly do not deserve it. And I doubt whether you are capable. Nevertheless, I will teach you the way to communicate *well*."

Crier rubbed his rough hands together. "All right then. Let's go. Tell me what to do to get this message off my hands. Show me *the* way and I'll be on *my* way home."

"Do not make light of this, son." Campazani looked at Crier sternly. "This is not easy. Understand something here: everybody communicates. Few communicate *well*."

Crier was only half listening, thinking instead about that first taste of good Zackovian ale. "Hm?"

"I said, 'everyone communicates'. For example, right now, you are communicating to me that you don't care at all about what I am saying. You just want to get this over with."

Crier blinked in surprise. "What are you, a wizard?"

"Yes. Yes I am."

"Oh. Right. Anyway, what do you mean, everyone communicates?"

"Well, stop and think about it. We, humans, were made to communicate. To interact, to talk, to...share. And, if you pay attention, you begin to realize that much of our lives are spent doing this. Sometimes we use words; sometimes we use just our eyes, our bodies, our hands, and so on." A look of sadness crossed the old man's face. "The problem is so many of us do it so poorly."

Crier stifled a small yawn. "So?"

"So? So?! Why do you think disagreements happen? Why do you think wars begin? It's not always greed and hatred. Sometimes, it's just...bad communication."

Crier raised his eyebrows. "Huh. I never thought of that."

Campazani gripped his arm tightly. "There is so much at stake here, my boy. And this is exactly why *you* must learn to communicate *well*."

He began to busy himself around the shop. "Communicating well requires a mix, a balance, of six elements. All six are necessary. Each in the proper proportion! Only then can you truly deliver the message to the queen."

"A whole bunch of—what do you call them?— elements? Six, you say?" Crier squinched up his nose as if catching a whiff of a bad smell. "Let's just start with the first one, eh, old man? That should be enough."

Campazani looked at him with a hint of disappointment in his eyes. If Crier noticed it, it didn't seem to matter to him. "As you wish, Crier." Crier smiled. *Just enough to get me on my way home!*

The wizard shuffled over to a dusty old cabinet, pulled out a vial of liquid, and held it up to the light. It was deep blue in color. He poured some into a cup and talked as he stirred.

"The queen has a lot on her mind. From dawn to dusk, she is bombarded with hundreds of people delivering hundreds of messages. How many of those people, do you suppose, give any thought to *the person* they are talking to? Do they even consider the royal audience in front of them? Their thoughts are only for themselves—for what the queen can give them, never what *they* are giving the queen."

He continued, as if to himself. "And Hesston, constantly at her side, filling her ears with poison..." He shook his head and turned to Crier.

"Now. First things first. Most Messengers are infected with a horrible notion. They think it is...about them. Crier, it is not about you at all."

Crier eyed the blue liquid warily. The wizard looked hard at him. "You understand what I am saying here? *It is not about you.*"

"What? Not about me?" Crier said incredulously. "What do you mean? It's *my* message, right? It's up to her to listen to *me!*"

Campazani shook his head emphatically. "No. Communicating well begins, not with the message, or even with the Messenger. It begins with the *audience.*

And that is why the first element you must possess is...*to be*."

"To what?"

"To be."

"To be...what?"

"To be...the audience you speak to."

Crier shook his head in exasperation. "Good Lord, man! What in heaven's name are you talking about?"

The wizard repeated himself. "You must *be* the audience you are speaking to." He smiled as if he were saying the simplest thing in the world.

Crier was slowly realizing this wizard might be missing a few elements of his own. "Alright, let's start over again, shall we?" He spoke with exaggerated slowness, as if talking to a child. "I...want...to...deliver...a...message...to...the...queen."

The wizard nodded impatiently. "That is what I am trying to teach you! Hm. Let's try another way. How about this? Crier, the first element you must possess is called *empathy*."

"Em-pa-thy," said Crier with a puzzled look on his face, as if this was the first time he had ever heard the word. And, in fact, it was.

The old man nodded as if reading his mind. "Empathy means, *putting yourself in the shoes of the other*. It is, unfortunately, one of the rarest emotions on earth. It doesn't come naturally. And very hard to learn! But thinking about 'the other' before yourself is the key to so many things in this life. And that is why the first element necessary to communicate well is *always* empathy." Campazani handed him the cup.

"Drink this."

Crier hesitated for a moment and then sighed. "Here's to a better pint tomorrow," he said and drained the cup. He shuddered. "Empathy. Yuck." He didn't like the taste of it at all.

As he put the glass down, he shook his head. He was feeling woozy. The old wizard's face swam in front of him, his voice echoing and throbbing. "Crier, what if you were a king?"

Crier mumbled through his haziness, "Ah, now you're talking, old man! Oh, how I would fill my days! Wine, women, and song! Women with wine, wine with women, singing songs about wine and women and..."

Crier blinked as a bright light appeared. Noise started to swell, but it wasn't noise from the shop or the street. A voice cut through. "Your Highness? Your Grace?"

Crier opened his eyes. He was looking out onto a vast, opulent throne room. All eyes were on him. He raised his arm and, with a gasp, saw he was dressed in robes of purple, covered in jewels and gold. He was seated on what was clearly a throne.

Before he could take all this in, the voice began again. "Your Highness? Are you ready to hear the next Messenger?"

He was staring into the eyes of the tall, burly palace entry guard. He blinked and tried to gather his bearings. Thinking back to what had just happened, he slowly realized that, somehow, the wizard's potion had transported him back to the throne room of Brynnland, except, wonder of wonders, HE was now the king!

He had to think quickly. He cleared his throat and said, "Carry...carry on then. Eek! Good God!"

The crowded room stirred uneasily. The "eek!" came out because he realized his voice sounded like a woman's, and the "Good God!" came as he touched his chest and felt...so much more there than usual. He wasn't a king after all. He was a—

"Madam?" He jerked his head to his right and saw Hesston staring warily. "Are you...fit to listen, my queen?"

Crier paused and quickly gathered himself (or was it herself? Egads!). Whatever magic this was, it was powerful. It wasn't just that he was in the place of the queen; he WAS the queen! It was absurd! How was this possible? But, as he looked around the room at the faces staring back at him, he realized that he'd better adjust to "being the queen," or he might lose his head as an imposter.

He opened his mouth and heard a woman's voice say, "Yes, Hesston. Of course. Proceed."

Hesston looked at Crier for a second longer. In that moment, Crier could see and feel the hatred, the deceit, and the ambition that flowed from the man beside him. *He hates her*, he realized with a start. *And this is her right-hand man, her confidant? How can she function like this, day after day?*

Crier tore his eyes from the smoldering gaze of Hesston and looked down, in front of the throne. He gasped in horror. Before him stood...himself! Crier was looking at...Crier! Him! "Good God!" Queen Crier said for a second time. He looked at the arrogant, sloppy, disinterested little man before him. He was speaking, but it was almost impossible to hear because he was mumbling. *Do I really look that bad?* He thought. *Do I really look so bored? He's—I'm—presenting to a queen!*

Crier (the queen) felt the eyes of the entire throne room upon him and heard the whispers as they waited for him to react. And Hesston was watching his every move. *What pressure to be under, at all times!*

His eyes came back to the little man before him. The frumpy figure had finished his "speech" and was bending down holding out the parchment expectantly. The nerve! Where was the respect for his audience? Anger began to build up in him, and he couldn't wait to send an arrow into this fool's hide. He raised his hand (admiring its delicate nails) and began to speak the order.

And then, without any warning, he was staring into the face of the old wizard. He was back in the dusty little shop. Disoriented, he stumbled and awkwardly plopped down on the wooden floor.

The wizard smiled. "It's a good thing I stopped you. You'd be sitting here right now recovering from not one, but *two* arrow wounds!"

Crier didn't say a word for a full minute. Campazani waited and then quizzed him.

"What about that Messenger? He walked into your throne room and expected you to pay attention to him."

Crier's face darkened. "Me? Pay attention to *him*? It's my attention! Why should I *pay* him any of it? The very idea that he even deserves my time! I'm a busy woman! I mean, man!"

The wizard nodded. "Exactly! Never forget how valuable someone's attention is. When it comes to delivering a message, your audience is the king and deserves the utmost respect. The audience is king. Or, in this case, the queen!" And he cackled at his little joke.

Crier rubbed his chin and thought about how it felt to *be* the queen. In a panic, he grabbed at his chest and then sighed in relief as he felt...the usual. The wizard continued.

"Element one. Empathy. *Be* the audience you are speaking to. Now, how should your message change?"

Crier thought for a long time. "Empathy means to imagine that I am the audience..." He squinted his green eyes. Even with the magic, he was having a hard time getting his mind around this strange new thought. He looked to the wizard. "So, you're saying that it's not about me. Right?" He walked around the little shop, thinking. "It's not about me." The fire crackled as a log shifted. The wizard watched as the moments ticked by.

Finally, Crier began to speak, slowly and deliberately.

"If it's not about me, then it is important to be thinking a great deal about the audience right from the start. Before I deliver a message, I need to be trying to understand who I am delivering it to. In this case, the queen." He nodded his head. "Who is this queen? How does the queen feel? If I understand more about her, I'll deliver the message differently."

Campazani nodded and turned around to clean up. Crier thought for a few more moments and then smiled as an idea popped into his head.

"Thanks, old man!" And with that, Crier raced out the door of the dusty shop.

He did not hear the little wizard calling him back.

Chapter
6

The next morning found Crier standing beside the guard at the door, waiting to enter the throne room. The guard looked at him and smirked. "Here to try it again, eh, foreigner? It'll be a painful experience, I guarantee you that!" He nudged him forward. "You're on."

Crier entered the bustling throne room, passed the bowman (who smiled as he followed him with his eyes), and walked to the throne. The queen was listening to Hesston as he talked and gestured. Crier took a moment to study her. He saw that same sad, faraway look in the queen's eye. *I understand what it's like to be her. I felt that!*

He looked at what she was wearing. *I wore that!* Still a fine figure, he had to admit. For a brief moment, Crier thought about his own appearance. He was glad he had taken the time to buy a new frock and run a comb

41

through his hair. Perhaps it doesn't hurt for a Messenger to be easier on the eyes, he thought. He looked around the ornate, crowded room, comparing himself to everyone else. Hmm. Maybe he should have given it even more thought.

Finally, the queen looked up from her conversation with Hesston. A small glimmer of recognition crossed her deep blue eyes.

She said simply, "The Crier of Zackovia."

Hesston stroked his neatly trimmed goatee and sat back studying Crier, thoughtfully. Crier looked at the menacing scar and the finely woven clothes and felt a stab of uncomfortable self-awareness. He made a mental note to visit Jack Tailor in Zackovia once he got done here. As Hesston's eyes bored into him, he wondered, *Is it more than the scar and the clothes? Is it possible he knows about the magic?* And with that terrifying thought, he cleared his throat to speak.

"Your Majesty," Crier began, "I appreciate you taking the time to hear me. I realize that I am asking you to *pay attention*, and I know that your time is worth so much. So again, thank you."

The queen looked thoughtfully at Crier and then made a slight movement of her head. Crier continued.

"I have spent some time walking the streets of your kingdom today, my lady. And I must say that the people I have come into contact with have been most kind to me. You must be proud of your subjects."

At these words, Crier noticed a sudden change come over the queen's face. It was as if a light came on behind her eyes. In that moment, Crier saw a much younger queen. And then, in a flash, the light went out, and she looked hard and old again.

"My people are all that matter to me," she said firmly.

Crier thought, *How would it feel to be loved like that?* Without thinking, he said, "I am sure they must appreciate having you as their queen."

The queen looked down and blushed. She busied herself with readjusting her dress. Hesston was watching the reaction with interest. Crier realized in surprise that it was *his words* that were causing these effects on the queen. Even more surprising, it made him feel good to see this. And, perhaps most surprising of all, he realized that he actually *meant* what he said!

What an odd thing, he thought to himself. *Empathy changes your message—and it changes the audience as well! And maybe, it even changes the Messenger.*

But this way of thinking was so foreign to him it hurt his head. So he brushed the memory of that powerful magic aside and thought instead about what came naturally: his own needs. He wanted to get back home, and soon. *Who needs more elements? It's as simple as knowing your audience and then giving them the message!*

Hesston pulled him back to reality as he snapped, "Quickly, Crier, before we lose patience."

With a nervous glance to Hesston, he continued. "Your Majesty, here is the message from my king. It is of the utmost importance. I know that it will be of great value to you. With respect and humbleness, may I offer it to you?"

Crier held the parchment out with bowed head, just as he imagined he would want to receive a message if he were the queen.

He waited. And waited. But the queen did not take the parchment.

After a long moment, the voice he heard was Hesston's, not the queen's.

"And what does the message *say*, Crier?"

"Hm? What's that?" Crier raised his head.

Hesston was leaning forward with a sly look. "This message of utmost importance. What does it *say*?"

Crier looked back and forth between Hesston and the queen. He stammered, "Er. Well, I did not actually read the message, Highness. I—"

Upon hearing this, the queen's face became a mask of coldness. Her voice began quietly and rose in volume as she spoke. "You come before me, again. You ask me to pay attention. And yet, you do not even care enough to know what the message *says*?"

Then she spoke quietly, as if to herself. "I almost believed you understood...." The queen's blue eyes burned. "If it is not important to *you*, Crier, how can it possibly be important to *me*?"

The queen herself made a quick motion with her hand.

Behind him, Crier heard an arrow being pulled from the quiver. As the bow stretched and creaked, Hesston's smirk widened into a smile.

Chapter

7

Crier slammed the broken arrow onto the table, causing Campazani to jump.

"I thought empathy was the key, eh?" Crier said angrily. "I understood that delivering this message wasn't about me—I mean, I really got it! I put myself in the queen's shoes, and she seemed to be really listening to me, right until the moment the arrow went into my—"

"Ah, my dear boy!" Campazani said. "Yes. Empathy is indeed the key. Communicating well *begins* with the understanding that it is not about you." The wizard waved a crooked finger. "But it is only the first step!"

Crier winced. "Right now it hurts to take any steps."

Campazani looked at Crier and cocked his head. "How did it feel, boy?"

Crier rubbed his bottom and said, "Well, it felt exactly like an arrow was shot into my—"

"No, no, you self-centered buffoon!" Campazani yelled. "When you looked into the queen's eyes, how did it feel?"

Crier sat down, winced, and frowned. It was always a hard thing to think about anything but himself. But then, he smiled.

He said, "It changed things. Especially when we talked about her people. It—it was as if a connection had been made, between us. I realized that I wasn't just giving a piece of parchment to a queen. I was sharing something with another person..."

Crier looked down and saw that he had joined his two hands together. It embarrassed him, and he quickly tried to separate them. But Campazani had leapt to his feet and wrapped his bony hands around Crier's.

"Yes! That is IT, boy. Empathy is what allows you to *connect* with your audience. It has its own special alchemy. You and the audience literally *share* the message." Campazani was beaming. "I am amazed. You are beginning to see!" He looked into the distance. "How she must have loved to hear some kind words."

Crier, basking in the praise, looked into the distance along with he wizard and said wistfully, "Yes. And if only I had read the message, just imagine how much better it could have been."

Campazani froze. Still holding Crier's hands, he shoved them into Crier's face, banging his nose so hard his eyes watered.

"What? You did not even READ it?!"

He let go of Crier's hands and stormed off. "For a moment there, I actually thought there was some hope. Good Lord, is there any chance that this will work?"

Crier rubbed his nose. "Okay, okay! Maybe I do need to learn some more about how to, um, communicate good. I mean, well." He thought back to those blue eyes and how it felt to see her face change because of *his* words. He wanted to see that again. "What else do I need to know?"

Campazani had his head down, as if in prayer. Finally, he sighed and went to the cupboard full of vials. They tinkled as he pulled one out and poured a cup of red liquid. "Now that you care about the queen, you must also care about the message."

He handed the little glass to Crier. "The second element...is Ownership."

Crier downed the liquid and grimaced slightly. "Huh?"

"Crier, you cannot simply take the message of someone else and hand it over, like you are passing the potatoes at dinner! That is not communication. Communication is making the message your own *before* you deliver it."

He took the empty glass and continued. "So many Messengers think that they can deceive their audience. They try to simply pass on someone else's words, or read from a prepared text. But they fool no one. People can tell immediately when you do not care about your words! They may appear to believe, but, when the Messenger walks away, the message is ignored. It is as if they had never spoken." The old wizard paused. "How tragic!"

Crier was still grimacing from the drink as Campazani said, "Ownership. You must own the message *passionately*."

The old wizard reached up and gripped Crier's vest tightly as he looked him in the eye. "Communication is about *passion*. If you don't care about what you are saying...don't say it!"

Crier shrugged. He wasn't convinced.

Campazani looked down at the faded flower pinned to Crier's vest. "You don't need this thing, do you? Why don't I throw it into the fire and—"

Quick as lightning, Crier pulled away, his eyes blazing. "That is mine. You have no idea what it means to me. Touch it again and—" He stopped as Campazani smiled.

"You care about that flower, do you? Why?"

Crier hesitated and then said quietly, "It's the only thing that was in my basket when the nuns found me on the doorstep. It's the only thing that's...mine."

Campazani nodded. "And that is how you must feel about a message that you deliver. You must care for it passionately. You must *own* it."

"You were chosen to deliver it—no one else. How can your audience care about something that you don't care about? It must be that important to you! Or it will never be important to the audience."

Crier was staring intently at the flower. The wizard continued. "Your audience will only care as much about your message as you do."

Crier was deep in thought. "Just like she said. It has to be important to me before it can be important to her."

He looked somewhat sheepishly at the wizard. "And to think that I did not even read it!"

"That is your flower, son. No one cares about it more than you." The wizard held up the parchment and smiled. "And this is *your* message. No one should care about it more than you."

Crier took the kingly parchment from the wizard, looking at it with a new respect.

"If I care about this, she will care. If I don't, she won't."

And with that, Crier sat down and cracked the royal seal, finally reading the message he had been chosen to share.

Mike Vayda

Chapter

8

The palace guard raised an eyebrow as Crier appeared once again at the door to the throne room of Queen Abigail of Brynnland.

"A *third* time, Crier? You seek yet *another* wound?" He smiled ruthlessly. "Perhaps you do not mind the pain. But surely we are tiring of the pain you are causing us!"

Crier glanced at him and mustered the best insult he could. "Oh really? Well...at least I am not causing to you the kind of pain you are causing to me with your FACE!"

The guard laughed. "Once again, your words reflect your intelligence. And you, Crier, are clearly a moron."

Crier was about to reply when the guard pushed him into the throne room.

"But at least you are a cleaner moron!" The guard called after him. Crier smiled, realizing that perhaps it was worth the two Cronin he had spent at John Barber's. His thinning hair had never looked so good.

As he walked, he looked around the room. People lined the red carpet that he walked on. If they cared at all to notice, they would see that the frumpy man was a bit less frumpy today. And he was walking with some sense of urgency. If appearance said anything, it said that Crier was on a mission.

He looked to the queen and noticed with a start that she was already looking at him. Their eyes met briefly, and he felt his heart flutter. Then the queen cleared her throat and in a formal voice said, "The Kingdom Crier."

Hesston, as always at the queen's side, touched the chain on his neck and smiled maliciously. "From tiny *Zackoooviah*, isn't it?"

A ripple of laughter ran through the room.

The queen raised a finger; the laughter cut off immediately.

Did he see a small amount of kindness in those blue eyes? He realized he had no idea what he wanted to say.

"Do you have a message for me?"

Crier blushed slightly, flustered. He shot a glance at Hesston. He was not smiling. Then he gathered himself and bowed.

"My lady, King Owin of Zackovia sends you warm greetings. But I am sorry to have to deliver to you some troubling news." He took a breath. He imagined how important this news would be to him in his own country and, in a loud voice, said, "Highness, there is great trouble coming to your kingdom!"

There was a short moment of silence. It was as if the crowded room was surprised to hear such a calm, strong voice from the little foreigner. Yesterday, they would have laughed him out of the room. Today, it was clear that the Crier meant the words that he said.

Finally, a murmur rose from behind him. He could make out several exclamations: "Impossible!", "Who is this little man?", "How dare he!", and "Who cut his hair?"

Crier tried to ignore the comments and took a step toward the queen. "With all respect, lady, your kingdom is in trouble! You must believe me!"

As Crier moved toward the queen, two guards on either side moved forward to block him with their spears. Abigail raised her hand, and the guards somewhat reluctantly pulled back to their positions.

Crier continued. "I read the message! And I see now that it is urgent news for you and your people!"

A look of concern crossed the queen's face. She paused and placed her fingers together in front of her. At last, she spoke. "What proof do you bring?"

Crier stared at her. "Proof? Proof?! I—I have none. But I am telling you, this message is true!"

The queen looked thoughtful. Every person in the room was looking to the queen before they reacted to this news. She looked into Crier's face. It was a bit touching—his new suit, his neatly parted hair, his green eyes pleading. But before she could speak, Hesston leapt to his feet.

"Why should we trust this tiny Zackovian toad? This is nothing but a trick!"

Hesston stepped down and began to circle him, gesturing and raising his voice theatrically. Crier turned his head to follow him.

"My good lady, this...foreigner shuffles into your throne room and yells like a maniac, 'You must listen! Oh, you must listen!'"

The room tittered. Then he looked back at the queen. "Surely it cannot be permitted that just anyone can get so close to the queen with these threatening words?"

He paced slowly before the throne room crowd. Gravely, he said, "We know how some women—in other courts, not this one—could be fooled if they were in some way...attracted...to a messenger."

A whisper ran through the room.

"But of course, we have no worries of such feminine weakness in *this* kingdom."

He let the words hang in the air. There was the smallest of murmurs in the crowd. Crier was watching the queen. To him, she suddenly appeared very alone.

She sat back, as if in defeat. She looked at Crier, at his green eyes silently pleading, and said softly, "I hear you, Crier. But, unless you can *show* me what you *tell* me, I cannot believe you."

Hesston made a small noise of triumph. Then he whirled dramatically and pointed toward the bowman.

Crier closed his eyes and waited for the pain.

As did the Queen.

Chapter
9

"**Well, thank you very much!**" Crier exclaimed as Campazani pulled the arrow from his forearm. The old wizard looked at Crier, surprised at his appreciation. Until he continued.

"Thank you, very much, for having me shot AGAIN by that blasted queen. All your words about 'owning the message passionately' got me nothing but another arrow in return. Ownership?! Well, I'm getting a bit tired of owning these wounds!" Crier sat on the table and fumed.

Campazani gently applied some salve to the flesh wound. "Son, I realize that you are in pain. And I commend you for putting into practice true empathy for the queen. I am also happy to hear that you showed passion for the message. But that is not enough. Not at all."

Crier stood up and grimaced. "Oh, *now* you tell me! After I have been shot not once, not twice, but

THREE TIMES as the Messenger. You have more pearls of wisdom, do you? Well please, do tell!"

With that, he thumped himself down into an old chair, dust flying. Coughing and wincing at the pain, he muttered, "You got me to care for her and her kingdom. But what good is it?" He pushed out his lower lip and pouted. "What good is it to care at all?"

The old wizard drew himself close to Crier, so close that Crier actually shrunk back in the chair.

"So. You care. Good for you. At last, you are concerned for someone beside yourself! That is certainly a monumental achievement for such a self-centered creature. But, answer me this, boy..." The wizard was now so close Crier could see the unruly hairs sprouting from his nose. "Why in God's name should she believe you?"

Campazani slowly walked around the chair, leaving Crier to twist and turn to follow him.

"All you need is to care, is that it? You think your audience should require nothing more than *good feelings* to believe every word you say?" He looked hard at Crier. "Then you really are a fool!"

He paused, and then he began again more gently. "My dear boy, I commend you for caring. It does my heart good to see such a selfish man begin to see the needs of a bigger world. Even if that world sits but on a single throne," he teased. Crier blushed. Campazani continued in a more serious voice.

"But *caring* is simply not enough. Communicating well is also about *convincing*. When in doubt, always go back to the first step. Imagine you are the queen. Would you be satisfied with what Crier said? Would *you* believe you?"

Crier thought for a moment. He shook his head reluctantly. "I guess I see your point. But what else do I have to do?"

Campazani continued. "You see my point? Excellent. The good news is that you have a point too."

"A point?" Crier stared dumbly at the parchment he was clutching. "What do you mean?"

Campazani reached into the drawer and pulled out a velvet bag. He opened it and spilled the contents onto the table. With a clatter, out poured dozens of stones and pebbles. Some were of value; most were not. A green jewel stood out, dazzling in its beauty. Campazani gestured to the pile.

"If this was your presentation to the queen, what would you want her to focus on?"

Crier looked at the wizard and frowned. He pointed to the green gem. "This one, obviously."

Campazani picked up the glittering jewel and held it in front of Crier. "THIS is your point. This is the single thing you want the queen to take away from your talk. I said that communicating well is about convincing. And it is always easier to do so when you have a singular goal, just one point to make." He put the stone back into the bag.

"First, you must be the audience you are speaking to. Second, you must own your message passionately. Third? *Prove* your point simply."

Crier frowned. "I understand proof. But, why simply? Why not provide dozens of reasons?"

Campazani pointed to the pile of stones. "One of the biggest mistakes Messengers make is trying to say too much. They try to put too many valuable things into the bag! Audiences are expected to take too much away, and instead, they leave with nothing. One takeaway. No more."

He pushed the other stones and pebbles out of the way and placed the bag with the single stone on the table. "King Owin has already provided you with a single subject, a takeaway, for your message. What is it?"

Crier shrugged. "The kingdom is in trouble."

Campazani nodded. "Good. The key now is to add other information, but only if it supports that point."

He went to his cupboard. "An audience is smart, and they are skeptical. Passion without evidence is nothing but hot air." He moved some vials around as he talked, until he found the one he wanted. "You must do more than care. You must have more than passion." He held up a vial of thick, inky liquid and squinted at it. He poured a small amount and thrust the glass at Crier. "First, you care. Second, you own. Now, you must PROVE."

Crier took the glass, sighed and raised it to his lips. The thick liquid moved like black syrup into his mouth. He shuddered. "That is such a strong taste!"

The old man nodded. "There is none stronger." As Crier emptied the glass, he continued. "You tell the queen she is in trouble. But have you explained *why*? Where is your evidence?" He gestured to the table. "What are your other rocks?"

Crier swallowed again, deep in thought as Campazani continued. "If you expect an audience to believe your message, you must give them *reasons* to believe."

Crier nodded in understanding. "Alright. I need to give her some proof." He looked at the old man. "How much proof do I need?"

The wizard slowly picked out three other gemstones from the pile and set them next to the bag. "There is some strange magic in the number *three*. It seems that people can readily grasp that amount. More than that can overwhelm an audience. Less than that and it will not be enough." He put the three stones into the bag, pulled the cord tight, and dropped the bag onto the table. "One takeaway. Three reasons."

Campazani walked to the cupboard to replace the vial. "And always remember—empathy! If you were her, what would convince you?"

Crier, already at the door, paused, nodded thoughtfully, and went out.

"And present them well!"

Chapter
10

Several days passed before Crier was once again waiting outside the throne room. The entry guard wrinkled his nose. "Have you been staying with friends, Crier?"

Crier was mouthing some words, obviously trying to remember something important. "Hm? What's that?"

"You smell hideous, and you look like you've been sleeping in a barn. I can only surmise that you have been staying with your friends: the farm animals."

Crier stopped moving his lips long enough to glare in the guard's direction. "You think you're funny, but you're not. For your information, I have been to the Borders these past few days." He smiled triumphantly. "I found a way around you and the soldiers!"

It hadn't been easy. He had paid a departing wool merchant for a ride in his cart in order to slip past the watchful eyes of Hesston's men.

"The Borders?" The guard looked at him warily. "Why on earth would you go all that way...and come back? If you were smart, you'd have just kept on going. Instead," and here the guard could not disguise a small flicker of puzzlement, "here you are again for more punishment."

He glanced at the throne room and said, "I warn you, dullard; deliver another message as you have thrice already, and you'll be lucky to walk out of that room under your own power!" He gave a shove forward to Crier, though not too roughly.

"Now do a better job, will you? I have no desire to dirty my uniform with your blood."

As he made the long walk to the throne, Crier noticed that there were even more people in the room than last time. Clusters of well-dressed people stared and whispered. The bowman leered, as if trying to decide where the next missile should be directed.

Two guards were dragging a court jester past him. The jester was whimpering from an arrow sticking out of his hand. As they passed Crier, one of the guards said, "How many times do we have to tell you? No mimes, no jugglers!" *Tough room*, Crier thought. He swallowed hard and approached the throne.

The queen watched the disheveled man walk toward her. Crier's haircut was now wasted; unruly tufts of red hair were matted with sweat. His face and body were caked with mud, hay, and stray bits of food. There were more than a few whispers about the audacity of appearing before the queen in this condition. Bets were quietly exchanged on how quickly the arrow would fly.

Hesston jumped up gleefully. "*This* is how a foreigner appears before me—er, before the queen? Perhaps this is how you do things in *Zackoooviah*," a snicker ran through the crowd, "but in civilized societies, we actually *bathe* on occasion."

The queen motioned for Hesston to sit down, which he did, reluctantly.

"Now, Crier," the queen said as she leaned back in her chair. "I seem to remember you upsetting the room the last time you were here."

Hesston interrupted. "What foolishness do you have to say this time? Or, should I save us all the time and send the next arrow right now?"

"No, no!" Crier exclaimed, looking alarmed. "Please...wait, Your Highness. Let me gather my thoughts."

"Gather your *thoughts*? This should not take long at all," Hesston said loudly, and the room snickered.

Crier tried to ignore the laughter. Despite his appearance, his voice was strong and confident. He looked at the queen and smiled slightly. "Good Queen Abigail, I apologize for appearing in your throne room in this manner. But I have good reason. When I was last here, I warned you that your kingdom was in danger. And yet, I had no proof of what I said. I aim to make up for that today." Crier bowed.

Crier began to walk slowly back and forth in front of the queen. "I must be clear on this one point: your kingdom is indeed in trouble." Crier paused in front of the queen. "I understand that you need proof of that." He raised his arm and extended three fingers. "I have just returned from the far corners of your kingdom. And I saw three sights that have compelled me to come before you and tell you...the news is even more dire than I thought!"

There was a murmur of unrest throughout the crowd. Crier turned to look briefly at them, making eye contact with various people. *They really aren't so terrifying when I see them one by one*, he thought, and this realization filled him with encouragement. Suddenly, he caught his breath. Amid the sea of strange faces, he thought he saw one he recognized. It was a woman. *Where did he know that face?*

"Get on with your lies, toad!" Hesston called. The face was gone. Crier turned back to the front of the room, raised one grubby finger, and continued.

"On the Borders, in the neighboring kingdom of Jakedom, I saw a large force beginning to assemble. Horses, weaponry, and many men with armor of strange marking. They are not from Jakedom, but they are amassing within that kingdom. And the force is moving toward your border!"

The room again was filled with murmurs and Hesston's loud voice exploded. "Impossible!

"I am sorry for the outburst, lady, but Jakedom is one of our fiercest allies—more so than the kingdom from whence this savage comes. I do not believe it!"

Crier looked darkly at Hesston before continuing. "It is true, dear queen. But I have even more proof to tell you," and he raised a second finger to the rafters. "I have seen your own army at its headquarters, and I am sorry to say it is lacking in both skill and motivation. Why, they simply sat and watched as merchants from Jakedom passed into Brynnland!"

Hesston broke in. "Lady, I myself manage our troops, as you well know. I can vouch for their readiness as always." The queen said nothing, her eyes fixed on Crier.

Crier ignored him and raised a third finger. "And finally, Your Highness, I walked into a shop set up and run by a Jakedomite—within your own kingdom! The man offered to sell me produce from Jakedom at a far cheaper price than your own crop in the very next store!"

Crier looked into the queen's blue eyes. "Dear lady, dark forces are working to take over your kingdom!"

At this, Hesston leapt to his feet, crossed the distance in a flash, and struck Crier across the face. The crowd gasped. As he struck Crier, the chain around his neck swung wildly. Crier saw a flash of metal before Hesston hastily hid the chain again among his garments.

Hesston was seething. "Liar! Spy! How *dare* you question the loyalty of our dearest ally!"

Crier's face stung, but he stood his ground. "It's true, my lady," he said quietly. "I saw it all myself."

Hesston scoffed. "Every charge you make against Jakedom, I deny on their behalf!" He looked at Crier with a condescending sneer. "And who are you that we should believe you? Your country can't even afford to raise a single horse and rider, and you think you are qualified to judge my skills as leader of an army?" He looked to the crowd. "Go back to the kingdom of idiots from whence you came, little man!"

"Sit down, Hesston." The queen said. The noisy room instantly became quiet. The queen stared hard at Crier. His eyes smarted, and his face burned from Hesston's glove. Though he wanted to look away, Crier matched the queen's gaze.

At last, she spoke.

"You have given me much to think about." She raised one hand to her mouth in thought. "If any of this is true, we would be wise to act." The queen paused again. "But, you arrive before me with mere words. Although they are convincing," here she glanced at Hesston, "words from a stranger are not enough to move me from my longstanding alliance with Jakedom. You say you saw it yourself. Perhaps." She searched the man's green eyes. "Perhaps. But I cannot see it."

Again the queen paused, as if making a difficult decision. "Almost you persuade me, Crier." She glanced again at Hesston. "But to believe a stranger over a friend would take more than mere words."

Immediately Hesston gestured to the bowman and leered at Crier.

"Make it hurt."

For Crier, knowing the queen did not believe him made it sting all the more.

Chapter

11

"But I saw it with my own eyes!"

The arrow clattered onto the floor. Campazani sighed and started dressing the latest wound. Crier barely seemed to notice the pain. "I went all the way to the Borders! I saw the guards look the other way as the merchants came through the open gates. I watched the army grow in Jakedom. I could have purchased the products myself if I wanted to. It is far, far worse than they know!"

Crier looked pleadingly at the wizard. "Why doesn't the queen listen to me? I found the proof! Three reasons! As plain as day! The queen should be welcoming me with open arms. Instead...she wounds me, again."

The old wizard stood thoughtfully, saying nothing. He could see that the freshly bathed little man really was hurting—and not just from the arrows. At last he shook his head. "Yes. You are right, Crier. Excellent research on your part! And three reasons—I commend you! Your proof should have been enough to convince the queen, or at the least, to move her to look into the matter herself. However, it is a sad fact that people will always believe what they already know rather than what they do not."

The wound bound, Crier grunted in pain and stood up. "Why? I don't understand."

"If the truth that is presented is unpleasant, people will go to great lengths to *not* believe it. Even if the truth is obvious, they will keep ignoring it as long as possible. Jakedom has been our most trusted ally since before this queen was born. It is not surprising she will not hear you."

As he talked, the old man walked to the closet and pulled out a vial. To Crier's disappointment, it was the same one containing the thick black liquid as last time. He watched warily.

"When the truth is unwanted, the Messenger must work all the harder to find a way to *make* it wanted."

He held the vial up. "To deliver a message, you must have proof. But proof is not enough. You must find ways to *show* the audience in a way they can see."

Crier looked doubtful. "Why? Why isn't the truth enough? Can't I just speak louder? Or repeat myself? Hey! What if I give them even more proof?"

Campazani held up the black bottle. "Fine. Are *you* ready for more of this? Would a gallon be enough?"

Crier winced. "Okay. I see your point. I don't need more proof. I just need to find ways to get her to see it. But how?"

Campazani was nodding as he revealed a second vial. This one was a small bottle of a many-colored liquid—bright orange, green, blue, yellow, and purple. The colors swirled, mixed and flowed. Crier watched with a great deal of interest as the wizard set the bottle down next to the first one.

"Let us face things, Crier," he said as he poured the black liquid into a glass and held it up. "Proof, by itself, is not attractive. It is not exciting. It is, you will remember, not easy to swallow. We need to find ways to make the truth...palatable."

He then added a small amount of the multicolored liquid. Slowly, the colors expanded and soon the glass was filled with swirling, sparkling colors. It looked delicious...mesmerizing. Crier was actually looking forward to drinking this one.

"You must *help* the audience see your proof. Eyes will remain closed until you make a way to open them." He held out the glass of beautiful liquid. "You show them the proof by adding the fourth element: Creativity. Now, drink this."

Crier didn't need to be told twice. He reached quickly for the vial and drank it all. He smiled and smacked his lips. His eyes were shining. "Creativity, eh? Ha! Wonderful stuff!"

The old man nodded and turned to place the dark liquid back into the cabinet. Crier looked longingly at the glowing vial still on the counter as Campazani continued.

"Wonderful stuff indeed. It is one of the most powerful gifts we have been given. With it, we have the ability to present proof in a way that will attract any audience *to* it. Creativity works hand in hand with empathy. If you know the audience well, creativity equips you to show them the proof in a way that they can understand. Start with the truth, and mix in the proper amount of creativity so that your queen will *want* to listen."

As the wizard continued talking with his back turned, Crier subtly reached for the vial of liquid on the counter.

"The message can be the same, but HOW you present it must be unique to each audience. That is the essence of creativity. It is used to flavor the message to properly suit the palate of each audience. Now—"

"Aaagh!"

Startled, Campazani turned to see Crier frantically reaching for a bucket of water. He buried his face into the bucket, spilling the water all over himself as he drank.

The old wizard waited, a bemused look on his face. At last Crier put the bucket down. He had a look of disgust on his face. It appeared he was keeping himself from throwing up only with great effort.

Campazani smiled. "As the queen has already shown you, proof without creativity is hard to swallow. But creativity without the truth? Ah. That is far worse."

The old wizard carefully capped the vial, and as he turned to put the powerful liquid away, he said, "Crier, use creativity to show the proof. Do whatever it takes, but by all means...."

Crier, who had been successfully fighting the urge to be sick, lost the battle and sprinted for the door.

Campazani yelled, "...use the right proportions!"

Chapter
12

The entry guard gaped as the menagerie paraded past him into the throne room.

"What in the name of—?"

He stared slack-jawed as Crier walked past him yelling, "Make way! Make way! Make way for the greatest message you will ever see!"

Crier winked confidently at the guard and said, "NOW the queen will get the point!"

The guard shook his head as a horse clopped past him into the room. He sighed and said, "No, Crier, I think it is *you* who will get the point—again!"

People jumped back and yelled in protest as he led his procession down the red carpet. The queen merely sat quietly with one raised eyebrow. It was clear that she was having a hard time believing what she was seeing. Finally, Crier arrived at the front of the room. There he stood, looking quite dapper. She was impressed at this, but it was what he had with him that was causing the entire throne room to buzz with excitement. Crier had brought a horse, a mongrel dog, and a sack with him. The horse was tied to a rope, which Crier was holding. Frankly, she didn't know whether to order him thrown directly into prison or see where this was heading. Intrigued, she decided to sit back and wait.

Crier was talking loudly, but it was hard to hear over the furor. She realized he had been talking for a while already. "...so you see, Majesty, this small horse is clearly, um, showing that—"

Crier glanced at the horse quickly before continuing. The little animal was obviously uncomfortable in the opulent surroundings and skittish in the crowd, and he began pulling away from Crier. It was soon apparent to everyone else that the animal was trying to find a place to relieve himself.

Crier, focusing on the queen, was unaware of this and tugged back on the rope. "This horse represents the power of your kingdom, and this wild, vicious dog here—"

Crier gestured to the mutt at his feet. The puppy scratched himself furiously, lost his balance and sat down in a clump. He cocked his head at the queen, and she had a hard time suppressing a smile.

"—This ferocious dog represents the kingdom of Jakedom, who was once a friend...your *best* friend...but now is trying to bite at your, um, heels and cause you problems. Vicious dog!"

The murmurs from the crowd increased. Hesston, who had arrived late, merely sat back and smiled.

With one hand, Crier held onto the rope and the leash of the animals, while with the other he reached into the sack and pulled out a looking glass. The pony continued to stir restlessly. The dog hacked up some grass.

He dramatically thrust the mirror in the direction of Hesston and yelled, "And you, Hesston! Look into this glass and what do you see?"

Hesston merely smirked and said nothing. After a moment of silence, Crier said, "...well, if you ask me, I see someone who is...er...pretty mean to foreigners for one thing! And not very trustworthy on top of that. Look! Do you see?!"

Hesston chuckled.

Sweating, Crier gestured dramatically to the dog. "And it is clear that Jakedom the dog knows this too!"

But the dog had his face buried between his legs, unaware of the performance he was part of.

The horse whinnied and slowly moved in front of Crier. Crier tried to push it out of the way so that he could see the queen clearly for his big finish. The horse stubbornly refused to move, forcing Crier to look over its shoulder. Hesston was enjoying this.

"...and in conclusion, Your Highness, I urge you to act on my message of warning. If not, I am afraid that—that—"

And here, Crier reached into the sack and theatrically produced a piece of paper currency. He held the bill up to a nearby candle. And waited. "I am afraid that...."

But the bill did not catch fire. Instead, it began to smolder, sending a large amount of acrid smoke into Crier's face. He began to cough.

"If not <*cough*> if you do not <*cough*> heed my warning, you will see the wealth of your kingdom go up in <*cough*> flames, like this bill is—well, should be..."

Finally, the currency caught fire. Crier yelped in pain as he dropped the flaming bill to the ground, but not before the flame spread to his new shirt. As he flapped at the flame, he lost his grip on the mirror, and it too fell with a loud crash, shattering into a hundred pieces.

This caused the dog to jump up, lift his leg, and neatly extinguish the small fire. More smoke was sent into the air.

The little horse looked down, as if remembering something important, and proceeded to relieve himself as well. On Crier's feet.

The entire court, which had been trying to contain itself, burst into peals of laughter. The pony began to neigh, the dog barked, and Crier could say nothing more. The queen looked at the dog and the pony, the smoke and the shards of mirror, and then she settled her eyes on Crier.

As the smell wafted up from his feet, Crier felt the terrible weight of the disaster. He stared at the little dog, trying to block out the chaos around him. Chaos that HE had caused. Vaguely, he heard Hesston arguing with the queen; he heard the mocking laughter as if from a long way off. He wished that he was the mongrel looking up at him, so he could run out of the room and never come back.

He heard Hesston talking loudly and realized the words were for him.

"I will give you a moment to make peace with your creator. And then? It will be time to say goodbye—once and for all."

Crier looked up at the queen and into the depth of her blue eyes. For a brief moment, he thought he saw a look of pity. Then, ashamed, he closed his.

He sighed. *Why did I ever agree to deliver this message? I should have told the king no.*

Hesston rose again to his feet and yelled with glee, "Bowman! Now!"

Crier was surprised at how quickly the pony could move out of the way when it wanted to.

Mike Vayda

Chapter
13

Crier sat, once again, on the table of Campazani, staring at the arrow in his hand, just recently removed from his hide. Crier threw it in disgust, and it clattered onto the pile of others.

The old wizard was speaking in a concerned voice. "My boy, you cannot afford any more of these wounds, do you understand?" Crier nodded numbly. "Hesston's order was to shoot to kill! You were lucky that mongrel bit the bowman's leg. It threw off his aim. Otherwise..." The wizard shook his head.

Campazani paused to look at the little man. He appeared beaten, broken. Had he ever seen someone come so far, try so hard to become a Messenger? Now was not the time for scolding—no matter how much of a disaster it was. *There might still be a way*, he thought. He sat down next to Crier and spoke softly.

"Crier, do you remember how sickening the taste of creativity was alone, without any truth?" Crier nodded glumly. A gag reaction overcame him for a moment. "That is similar to how your presentation must have felt to the queen."

"But why?" Crier asked. "I thought my examples were very creative."

"Creative?" The wizard thought for a moment and smiled. "In a manner of speaking, yes. But—and look here Crier, for this is so very important—creativity is never the point. When you seek to communicate, *creativity must always be a servant to the message, never the master.*" Crier looked dazed. "Crier! Did you hear what I said?"

Crier blinked. He sighed and repeated, "Creativity is the servant of the message, never the master."

Campazani continued, "I am certain that, had you kept the proper order of the two, you never would have used the animals or the props that you did. They did very little to enhance the message. In fact, they made the message harder to find!"

Crier nodded again, reluctantly.

"You cannot simply be *creative* and expect it to be *effective*. Creativity is such a powerful force. It must be harnessed—like your pony!—or it will overwhelm the very information you are trying to share." He grimaced at the sight of Crier's boots. "Like your pony."

Crier sat at the table and thought for a long time about his presentation. Slowly, he said, "So, are you saying that having a dog and pony show doesn't guarantee a better message?"

Campazani shook his head. "Nor does using smoke and mirrors, my boy. Creativity is so strong, so wild!

There is only one way to make sure it doesn't overwhelm your message: practice and preparation."

He stood up and changed his tone of voice. "Practice, preparation, discipline...these are all part of the fifth element of communicating well." He waited until Crier looked up before continuing. "The fifth element is the art of delivering all the other elements in proper proportion. The fifth element is *Give*."

Crier looked up. "Give? Just give?"

"Give *compellingly*," Campazani stressed. "Think of your message as a gift to someone you love." He looked at Crier. "That isn't hard to imagine, is it?" Crier colored. "This element is about gathering up all you have—empathy, passion, proof, creativity—and delivering it all in such a way that your audience has no choice but to believe you!"

"Sounds simple enough," muttered Crier.

"Ah, but it's not. Not at all! In some ways, this element demands the most work of all."

He looked out his window. Recently he had done some cleaning and now could watch the life passing by outside his shop. He looked thoughtfully at a young mother playing with her little baby. After a long moment, he continued. "Think of a message...as a child being born. Conceiving the idea is only the beginning! It takes a great deal of time to form and grow and then finally birth. It takes effort." He saw Crier sucking on his burned fingers and smiled. "Yes, and pain as well."

"All the previous elements are like the months of pregnancy. To *give* is to take the time to prepare for a successful delivery. It all comes down to this!"

He watched Crier for a long time, his eyes softening. He said quietly, "My Lord! Your own mother went through so much—" Here he caught himself. "Er, must have gone through so much to deliver you!"

Crier instantly came out of his funk. "My mother? What are you talking about? Did you know my mother?"

Campazani turned away. He looked out the window at the woman as she held the baby up in the air, both laughing. Finally, he shrugged, as if making a sudden decision he wasn't planning on. "Yes, I know your mother. She is a wonderful woman."

Crier jumped to his feet. "*Know? Is?* Are you saying that she's—"

"Alive?" Campazani took off his spectacles to clean them. "Oh yes, my boy. Yes she is. In fact, you met her."

"When? Where?" Crier was breathless. *How could it be?*

"The night in the pub, when the king summoned you. Do you remember?"

Crier thought back. "Yes...a woman sitting at the bar...staring at me! My...God..." He slumped into a chair, overwhelmed at the thought.

"And she has been reporting back to me your adventures in the throne room as well." Crier thought back to the face he saw in the crowd a few days ago. It was too much to take in! Campazani knelt in front of him. "Son, listen carefully to me. Are you listening?"

Crier slowly looked at him and nodded. Campazani took a breath and began.

"Your mother arriving in Zackovia, on that night, at that time, was the culmination of a plan that was put into place a long, long time ago. In fact, the night you were born! You've grown up thinking you were an abandoned orphan. Nothing could be further from the truth! The reason you were taken to Zackovia in the first place was to protect you. If not for the help of King Owin, you, and your mother, would have been killed many years ago."

Crier continued to sit, not saying a word. He was overwhelmed at the words he was hearing. Campazani went on. "Oh—there is so much to tell you! About the three kingdoms of Zackovia, Brynnland, and Jakedom...about your father, about what happened the night you were born, how the Messengers were broken...about the dark forces even now gathering..."

"Tell me!"

Campazani pulled Crier to his feet. "There is no time. Look here!"

Crier stared at the old man. "Son, I will tell you...but not now. Not when so much hangs in the balance. *Everything* depends on this message. Time is critical. You must convince Queen Abigail, or it will be too late. And all these years of waiting and planning and hiding and sacrifice will have been for nothing! You simply *must* give this message well."

Crier was dazed at the incredible revelation, but he shook his head, as if to clear it. Campazani's heart leapt. He saw a new fire in Crier's eyes.

"Alright. Tell me how to give a message compellingly."

Campazani nodded. "Good. As I said, it is in many ways the hardest, most important element. Yet it is so often ignored!" He shook his head and snorted in disgust. "I will never understand this idea of 'winging it!' A successful presentation is more than just the words. It is a mystical combination of message *and* Messenger. Anyone who thinks he is a Messenger without a lot of practice *giving* it is bound to be wearing an arrow or two. He deserves them!"

Crier thought for a moment. "So...I am guessing that you have no potion to help me."

Campazani smiled. "That is correct. Giving the message is, by definition, work!"

Crier took a breath. With a somber look, he said, "Campazani. You have taught me to be the audience I speak to, to own the message, to prove my point simply, and to show the proof creatively."

Campazani watched him closely as he continued.

"I understand so much more now. But I need help. I can't afford another dog and pony show! I know I can't get by with smoke and mirrors! I promise to work hard, but I need you to help guide me to combine all these elements. I'm not asking you to give the message for me. But I am asking for help so that I may give it *well*. Will you? Help me?"

Campazani smiled. "You are not the first Messenger in your family to ask for help." He took a breath. "Time is very short. Let's begin."

Over the next three days, people walking by the shop reported that voices could be heard through all hours of the night.

Chapter
14

Queen Abigail of Brynnland looked thoughtfully at the man standing before her. This was not the same arrogant, surly, unkempt foreigner that first waltzed in two weeks before.

Crier was wearing a new, stylish set of clothes. He had trimmed that awful beard and the unruly mass of thinning hair was pulled back into a ponytail. And he had bathed! *In the right light, he may even be considered a bit handsome*, she thought to herself. She had to work hard to hold back a smile. Meanwhile, Hesston was sitting with a puzzled look on his face. As Crier approached, she collected herself and said sternly, "The only reason you are standing here, Crier, is because of the great respect my father had for the man standing next to you."

The wizard Campazani stepped forward and bowed. "I am grateful for your favor, lady. I have not seen you since you were a child, but I perceive the strength of King Leonard in you."

A look of pride crossed the queen's face. "I do not know you. But my father left word before he died, should Campazani request anything, I should never deny him. An audience with me is the least I can do for someone my father so admired."

Hesston suddenly leapt to his feet, and, reaching for his sword, screamed, "It IS you!"

Campazani turned to Hesston and stood his ground. He calmly said, "Ah, you must be Hesston, correct? I don't believe we have ever met."

Hesston hesitated, sword in hand, scar burning.

Campazani continued. "For, if we had," he paused and glanced at the queen, "it must have been many, many years ago. I have not been in the throne room for ages. Why, the last time I was here was that terrible day when our king—the queen's father—suddenly took ill and died."

He looked at Hesston.

"You would not have been here on *that* day, would you, sir?"

Hesston had not moved. He looked from Campazani to the queen and then to Crier. Slowly, he slid the sword into the scabbard and eased back into his seat. "I must be mistaken. I thought you were an old…acquaintance of mine."

He looked back at the queen, who had been watching him closely, and smiled. "Of course, I did not step foot in this country until *after* we heard the news of King Leonard's untimely death. You will recall that Jakedom sent me to help with the transition."

He looked at Abigail with what he wanted to be a kind look. "Thank goodness your father made preparations for us to help advise you before he died. As you know, my dear queen, you were just a little girl at the time."

"And, yet, here you are. *Still?*" muttered Crier. The queen quickly looked at him.

Hesston shot a glance at Crier as well. Turning to the queen, he took her hand. "This brings back so many memories of our long and prosperous relationship. Although I do not know this man," he gestured vaguely toward Campazani, "if he is bringing any ill news of our friends, I would strongly suggest that the queen not bother herself with his words. In fact, I am surprised that you allowed him in this room. Your father, may he rest in peace, surely could not have meant to hold you to a promise for so long a time?"

The queen looked at Hesston. "And yet, you are still here...for so long a time."

Hesston colored slightly and removed his hand to gesture wildly at Crier. "As Chief Advisor to Your Highness, I really must insist that we dismiss this...foreign instigator...and anyone he has brought with him, immediately! He has had more than enough chances to deliver a message. He has failed. Guards!"

The guards began to move toward Crier and Campazani, swords drawn.

"Stay your hand."

The queen's voice was soft and strong. The guards stopped in a moment of indecision. Then they returned to their positions. The crowded room was deathly silent. This was amazing theater.

The queen glanced from Crier to Campazani. She turned to Hesston. "Thank you, as always, for your advisement, counselor. Now, I will advise *you* to sit silently. I will hear what this man has to say."

Hesston opened his mouth as if to reply and then sat back, stroking his beard and glowering at Campazani.

The queen turned to Crier. "The company you keep speaks volumes in the place of your own words. This man next to you has earned you the right to one more try. Now, my Kingdom Crier," she said, a tiny twinkle in her blue eyes, "what is your message?"

Crier looked around him at the crowded throne room, which had been absolutely silent throughout the course of this extraordinary episode. He turned and saw the bowman, standing with a cruel smile of anticipation on his face.

He looked back at the entry door and gestured to the guard. The guard nodded and disappeared. He reappeared ushering in three people: a woman master artisan, a soldier, and a farmer. As the three walked past him, the guard caught Crier's eye and gave the slightest of nods. Crier nodded in return and turned to Campazani.

The little wizard handed Crier a few items and looked up into his eyes. He said fiercely, "You were born for this."

He shuffled away. Crier took a deep breath and began.

Over the next fifteen minutes, the good-for-nothing Kingdom Crier from a backwater province masterfully delivered his message.

He brought forth maps and pointed out exactly where the troops were gathering on the borders. He presented various goods and currency to show that foreign trade was being conducted illegally within the borders of Brynnland. And, one by one, he presented the artisan, the soldier, and the farmer as eyewitnesses.

Each firmly verified that, indeed, these things were true. Finally, Crier ended his message with a confident review of the evidence and all that he knew.

Then, he was finished. He bowed his head to the queen and waited.

The room sat in stunned silence. Not a word was spoken; not a sound was made.

The queen leaned forward on her throne. She looked very troubled. She stared at the ground for a long time, and the silence continued.

Suddenly, Hesston leapt to his feet. "How dare you! I say arrest this man! He should be taken immediately to the guillotine and—"

The queen raised one hand, and Hesston stopped short. He began again more quietly.

"Good queen, I am concerned that—"

She said quietly, "Enough, Hesston."

"But my dear girl, it is clear that—"

"ENOUGH!" The queen spat, fire in her blue eyes.

Hesston, though clearly seething, sat down. Still looking at Hesston, Abigail said quietly, "I believe you now, Crier. You have convinced me."

Crier breathed a sigh. *It was over!*

Then the queen looked at Crier, almost imploringly.

"What do we do?"

Crier was stunned.

What do we do?

He was prepared to answer any question, to counter any argument against his message. But he was not prepared for this.

"Highness. I...Highness, I do not know."

The queen looked into his eyes. "Crier. You deliver a powerful, troubling message, yet you do not deliver a solution." The queen held out her hands. "What good is believing this unless you can offer me a way out?"

Crier tried to think of something to say.

"You have left us all far, far worse than when you came."

The queen stood and slowly walked in front of her throne. "My people," she said quietly, almost to herself. It was the first time Crier had seen her stand. In fact, it was the first time anyone in the crowded room had ever seen her off the throne.

"I have done," she gestured vaguely in the direction of Hesston, "all this...for my people."

She looked at Campazani and then at Crier. She laughed bitterly. "I have spent...my life...in this room, agreeing to what I have been told, in hopes that it was saving this good kingdom from destruction. And now, I see that instead, I have been spending my life doing just the opposite. What a fool I have been. What a fool."

She looked at Crier. Suddenly he saw, not a fierce, bitter woman but a beautiful, frightened girl, who for years had been surrounded by strangers and enemies. She smiled sadly. "Thank you Crier. You have delivered your message. You may leave."

Behind Crier, the bowman looked expectantly at the queen, his fingers resting lightly on the bow and arrow.

But the queen merely shook her head slightly.

"Leave me, Crier," she sighed.

He didn't know what to say. Reluctantly he turned from the queen to go. As he walked out of the silent room, Crier saw the faces looking helplessly back at him. He felt the queen standing behind him, watching him.

This pain, thought Crier, *is worst of all.*

Mike Vayda

Chapter
15

"Something! Anything!"

Crier was pacing the floor of the old shop, mindlessly opening cabinets and fiddling with vials.

"Please! Don't you have anything to help me?"

Campazani slowly shook his head. "I am afraid I have nothing else to give you, son. There are six elements necessary to communicate well." He raised one finger at a time as he listed the things Crier had learned. "You have *empathy*. You *own* the message passionately. You found *proof*. You showed it *creatively*. And you *gave* the message compellingly." He held up his open hand and shrugged. "You have all I can give."

Crier suddenly stopped at a cupboard, looking troubled. "But...but you said there were six elements. That is only five! What is the sixth element?"

The old wizard smiled. "Ah. The final element. In the end, it is the most important and complex of all. But I cannot give you something to drink. I cannot train you in this skill."

Crier was puzzled. "Well...what is it? I can't believe you are unable to help me. But at least tell me what it is, and I'll do anything to find it."

Campazani just shook his head. "What is the sixth element? *You* must decide what it is. It can only come...from you."

He reached up and Crier winced slightly, awaiting a smack on his head. The little wizard smiled and put a gentle hand on Crier's face instead. "I am sorry, son. I don't have it. But you *can* find it. In fact Crier, I believe you already know it. Just...look around."

Crier looked at him and frowned. He walked slowly out of the old shop and into the street. The wizard watched him go. Quietly he murmured, "It is all up to you now."

Crier walked through the pleasant cobblestone streets of Brynnland.

All these people, he thought. *"My people,"* she had called them. *Unaware of their impending doom.* Doom that he reported but could not fix! His king would be so angry—possibly even punish him for his failure. But that hardly mattered to him. Crier's heart ached more for Queen Abigail and these good people.

These good people. Campazani said to look around. Crier took a seat at the fountain outside the cathedral. Even though Hesston had shut the cathedral doors long ago, this cheery square was still the heart of the kingdom. He watched the children race past him, laughing as they chased a little dog, barking happily. With a smile, he noticed it was the same mongrel that had saved his life in the throne room. He watched a shopkeeper bargain good-naturedly with his customer over fruits and vegetables. He put the produce in her sack in exchange for a few Cronin. Then, while the customer wasn't looking, he threw in a few extra potatoes.

Crier turned and saw a blacksmith, talking with a woman about the tool he was making for her. He was proud of his work, and it was obvious that the woman was grateful for the blacksmith's skill.

A young mother who was sewing a frock held it up against her daughter to compare the size. The little girl danced around, holding her gift. A neighbor smiled as she set a pie out to cool, a present for an ailing friend.

Watching all this, Crier was reminded of the people in his own kingdom of Zackovia. The thought was a sudden stone in his heart. Amidst the bustle of the street, he hung his head. Why had he treated them so badly over the years? What had they ever done to him? He remembered the cruel things he would think and say and how he would purposely do his job poorly.

He closed his eyes at the memories, shamed. How he regretted his actions, his intentions! As he sat among the people in the busy square, he decided that if he ever had the chance to be the Kingdom Crier again, he would do it very differently. He would be honored to be a Messenger to people like these.

He opened his eyes and looked around. But would he ever have the chance? What would happen now that Brynnland was on the verge of defeat? Would Zackovia be next?

He thought back, many days now, to that first audience with King Owin of Zackovia. He could see the scene so clearly. What an arrogant ass he had been! He recalled the king's command:

"Rest assured that it is you who must do this, son. No one else."

"Yes, of course, Your Highness," said Crier as he took the parchment. *"I will hand it to the queen...."*

"No, Crier," the king said, somewhat sternly. *"I said, 'Deliver it to her in the best manner possible.' Do you understand?"*

He looked up to see Patrick, the red-haired monk who had shown him the way to Campazani that first day. His arm was still in a sling. He was slipping some coins into a blind beggar's hand. A boy ran past Patrick, across the steps of the cathedral and down a small lane, a loaf of bread for his family in his arms. Crier paused, looked up to the sky, and then looked back at Patrick.

Suddenly, his eyes widened.

He smiled.

Ha. Of course! *The best manner possible.*

He jumped up and ran over to Patrick. Crier began to talk quietly, and the monk listened intently. He was silent for a few moments. Then, with a handshake, Crier headed for the castle as fast as his legs could carry him.

Chapter 16

The burly entry guard looked despondent.

"Crier, if you do not have a new message for us, we will perish."

Crier nodded thoughtfully. The guard motioned him forward.

"Then, proceed."

If the throne room had felt sad to him before, it was much worse today. It looked the same. The same large crowd. The bowman. Hesston. The queen. But the sadness was overwhelming now. No one moved. No one spoke. Just the sound of an occasional soft weeping.

Beautiful Queen Abigail looked up and, for a moment, a smile came across her face.

"Ah. Our Crier," she said, not unkindly. "Do you have another message for us? For if you do, I do not think that I can bear it. Or perhaps you have come to sit with us as we watch our kingdom come down?"

Crier stood silently before her as she continued.

"Our borders are being overrun, as you said. Our market is flooded with foreign goods, and we do not have the funds to battle against it. And our army?" Here she glanced at Hesston. "Our army seems unable to stand against Jakedom. Our old friend." Hesston did not meet her eyes. She laughed roughly. "Perhaps the dog and pony were telling us the truth after all."

Crier moved close to the queen. Hesston watched warily.

"Queen. Your Highness. Listen to me, if you please." Crier said gently. "I have stood before you six times already! When I first came, I was arrogant and ignorant, full of myself. Since then, I have learned...so much! I discovered what it means to be the audience...to care about you more than I care about my own self."

He paused and said shyly, "And I do. Care about you."

The queen smiled.

"I have learned that I must own my message passionately. And, oh, I care more about this message than anything!

"I have worked hard to prove the message simply...and to show you that proof creatively." He smiled. "Er, perhaps a bit too creatively. I have decided I will leave the smoke and mirrors out of my messages from now on." She laughed at the memory, and he loved the sound.

"And I have learned to give the message to you compellingly. In short, I have learned what a privilege it is to have you as my audience and to be a Messenger."

Hesston was struggling mightily to hear the intimate conversation, but he could not quite make out the words.

"And now, I think I understand the most important step of all." Crier leaned closer. "To deliver this message to you in the best manner possible, I have to be able to offer you a solution...a way to *change* your situation. For what good is a message if it does not change the audience in some good way?"

"Your Highness? May I be of assistance?" Hesston said, watching Crier intently.

The queen kept her eyes on Crier, as if Hesston never spoke. Crier continued. "And to do that—to change things—I have to offer you...myself. To deliver a message *in the best manner possible* is to do it as a servant, bringing good change."

Crier slowly got down on his knee. "Queen Abigail, all that I have, I offer up to your service. To deliver a message is not enough. The message must include the Messenger himself."

Hesston said loudly, "Highness, I really must object to this intimacy...."

The queen looked at Crier. Small tears stood in her blue eyes.

Crier said, "My lady, with your leave?"

The queen, puzzled, nodded her head.

Crier stood up and turned to Hesston, who had been leaning close, trying to hear. Crier faced the man for a moment. Hesston sneered. "What is it you want, you ugly little man? Tell me quickly before I have that bowman deliver the final blow that you've deserved all along, you pathetic—"

Crier, quick as lightning, reached out and yanked the chain from Hesston's neck. Hesston grabbed, but too late. As the room gasped, Crier opened up his hand and revealed, on the necklace, a single, shining key.

Crier turned slowly so that the entire room could see and hear. "This is the key to the doors of the cathedral. Hesston locked the doors years ago. But it was never about religion. Hesston locked the door to the sanctuary because that was where the people would meet and talk, where they would share ideas. Even more, he was locking the door to the tower, to the bells. In short, he was locking the doors on communication.

"Without the ability to share news freely with each other or with the outside world, Brynnland could be controlled until the time was ripe for conquest. That time is at hand."

He turned to the throne. "Queen, with your permission, I will take this key and unlock the doors of the cathedral. I will climb the steps and, at the top of the tower, I will ring the bells and cry out to your people to help me save the kingdom of Brynnland." The queen's blue eyes shone as she smiled and nodded.

The room sat in stunned silence. Crier continued with a strong voice. "Hesston has been a traitor to your kingdom. He has been communicating with the dark forces within Jakedom behind your back. Deal with him as you wish. My job is to finish delivering my message. The people the queen loves and serves must hear it as well."

He turned to Hesston, who was sitting, shocked, in his chair.

"And my king will hear the bells, and he will come with ten thousand men and ten thousand horses—already amassed at the border. And we will drive the enemy from this land." He smiled at the old man. "For my *Zackoooviah* is not nearly as weak as you think."

He took the hand of the queen, kissed it, and said, "Queen Abigail of Brynnland, thank you for the privilege of your attention."

Then, key in hand, Crier turned to walk out of the throne room. Suddenly, a gloved hand grasped desperately onto his arm. It was Hesston.

"Abigail! You must not listen to him!" Hesston's eyes were now pleading. "We do not need help. We can solve this problem on our own. Listen! I have a plan!"

Hesston stood holding onto Crier's arm, a fearful look on his face. "Give me a moment, and I will explain it to you. Listen to my words, not his! Hear me!"

Crier looked at the queen, who nodded. He shrugged the hand off his arm and looked at the bowman.

"Go ahead. Shoot the Messenger."

As he left the room, he heard the familiar sound of the bow being pulled back. But this time, it was not for him.

+ + +

Crier arrived at the cathedral and found Patrick and the monks waiting for him at the doors. He handed the key to Patrick. Smiling, Crier said in a sanctimonious voice, "Would not our Lord want me to help you in this way?" They both laughed, and with his good hand Patrick unlocked the dusty doors and swung them open. Crier quickly climbed the stairs to the tower. When he reached the top, he grabbed the rough rope and pulled with all his might.

The bells rang, long and loud. The sound poured out, over the square, through the cobblestone streets, past the shops and kingdom walls, and over the plains.

He turned and looked down into the upturned faces of the good people of Brynnland, gathering in the square. He saw little Campazani, a tear in his eye. Queen Abigail appeared, slipped her arm into the wizard's, looked up at him, and smiled a dazzling smile. Suddenly, the woman from the pub—his mother!— appeared on the other side of Campazani, her beautiful face beaming.

The last peal of the bells faded. He looked out to the hills and watched the cloud of dust rise from the oncoming army of Zackovia. Then the Kingdom Crier, in a loud, firm voice, began to present the news of the day.

He delivered it well.

The Six Elements of Communicating Well

It is not about you.

You must

1. **Be** the audience you speak to,

2. **Own** the message passionately,

3. **Prove** it simply,

4. **Show** it creatively,

5. **Give** it compellingly, and

6. **Change** the audience positively.

About the author

 **For over 25 years, Mike Vayda** has been helping people and organizations communicate their important stuff *well*. He has produced conferences, training programs, and media on five continents. Through **Vayda Productions**, he's worked with Fortune 500 companies, small businesses and academia. In 2008, he co-founded **NotFar.org**, a non-profit dedicated to helping humanitarian groups tell their stories, so people can get closer to poverty free, meaningful lives. He lives with his family in the cool college town of Oberlin, Ohio. He and his wife are trying to raise good kids, make a difference, and enjoy coffee in as many interesting places as possible.

Shoot Mike a message!

Shoot@VaydaPro.com

Also check out

www.VaydaPro.com

www.NotFar.org

Communicate Well!

**Mike Vayda is available
for speaking, consulting, training
and producing remarkably effective
conferences.**

For more information contact:

Shoot@VaydaPro.com

or check out

www.VaydaPro.com

www.NotFar.org

Made in the USA
Charleston, SC
11 May 2011